电子科技系列科普绘本
Serial Pop Science Picture Books on Electronic Sci-tech

你知道与不知道的 HOW MUCH DO YOU KNOW ABOUT

雷达 THE RADAR?

（中英对照版）
(Chinese-English Version)

赵轲 主编　　Written by: Ke Zhao

赵轲 龙梅 郝聪婷 翻译　　Translated by: Ke Zhao　Mei Long　Congting Hao

电子科技大学出版社
University of Electronic Science and Technology of China Press
·成都·

图书在版编目（CIP）数据

你知道与不知道的雷达：汉英对照 / 赵轲主编.
成都：成都电子科大出版社, 2024. 12. -- ISBN 978-7-5770-1481-4

Ⅰ. TN95-49

中国国家版本馆 CIP 数据核字第 2025PB0201 号

你知道与不知道的雷达（中英对照版）
NI ZHIDAO YU BUZHIDAO DE LEIDA (ZHONG-YING DUIZHAO BAN)
赵轲　主编

策划编辑	谢忠明　段　勇
责任编辑	蒋　伊
责任校对	段晓静
责任印制	段晓静

出版发行	电子科技大学出版社
	成都市一环路东一段 159 号电子信息产业大厦九楼　邮编 610051
主　页	www.uestcp.com.cn
服务电话	028-83203399
邮购电话	028-83201495
印　刷	成都久之印刷有限公司
成品尺寸	250 mm×250 mm
印　张	2
字　数	46 千字
版　次	2024 年 12 月第 1 版
印　次	2024 年 12 月第 1 次印刷
书　号	ISBN 978-7-5770-1481-4
定　价	36.00 元

版权所有，侵权必究

创作团队   CREATION TEAM

顾问 CONSULTANT

陈德利

Deli Chen

儿童顾问 CHILDREN CONSULTANT

陈昕悦

Xinyue Chen

作者 WRITER

赵 轲

Ke Zhao

创作人员 OTHER CREATORS

郝聪婷　　　王念慈　　　叶桂兰　　　韩徐源

Congting Hao　　Nianci Wang　　Guilan Ye　　Xuyuan Han

设计制作 DESIGNER

吴依诺　　　吴佩谦　　　宋天豪

Yinuo Wu　　Peiqian Wu　　Tianhao Song

AR 开发 AR DEVELOPER

苏州和云观博数字科技有限公司

Suzhou AR-Museum Digital Technology Co., Ltd.

AR 读本这样用
How to Use the AR Books?

1. 用手机或平板扫描上方二维码，下载"云观博"APP。
Scan the QR code with your smart phones or pads, and download the "AR-Museum" app.

2. 选择"社教"中的"电子科技博物馆AR读本"，点击"AR"功能。
Select "the Electronic Science and Technology Museum AR Books" in "Social Education" Section, click the "AR".

3. 扫描部分页面中的""（小眼睛图标）。
Scan the icon " " on some pages.

4. 看图片、听语音、玩转3D，还有精彩视频，让你全方位了解这件了不起的发明。
Find more about the amazing invention with pictures, audios and 3D videos.

人物简介
Introduction of Characters

姓名：沃森·瓦特
身份：英国物理学家、雷达技术专家，世界上第一个实用雷达系统的设计者

Name: Watson Watt
Identity: British physicist, expert in radar technology, designer of world's first practical radar system

姓名：小科
身份：6岁的小男孩
性格：充满好奇，喜欢探索和提问，喜欢电子科技产品

Name: Kyle
Identity: Six-year-old boy
Character: Curious, like to explore and ask questions, fond of electronic products

序章：进入雷达世界
INTRODUCTION: ENTERING THE WORLD OF RADAR

天气预报是怎么预知天气的呢？

How does weather forecasts predict the weather?

今晚有雨，请带好雨伞！
It will rain this evening. Don't forget your umbrella!

这天，小科来到电子科技博物馆后，手机突然播报起了明天的天气情况。

One day, when Kyle is visiting the Electronic Science and Technology Museum, the weather forecast appears on his mobile phone screen.

和我一起去雷达世界看看，就知道了！

Come with me to the world of radar. Then you'll see.

　　天气预报就是通过雷达进行大气探测后，分析所得出的结果。雷达是一种用电磁波探测和定位目标的电子设备，被广泛应用于气象预报、环境监测、资源探测、军事装备等各个领域。

Radar detects the atmosphere and makes analyses. Then we get the weather forecast. Radar is an electronic device. It detects and locates targets with electromagnetic waves. It's widely used in fields such as weather forecasting, environment monitoring, resources detecting and military equipment.

雷达的发明
INVENTION OF RADAR

詹姆斯·克拉克·麦克斯韦发现了电与磁之间的联系并预言了电磁波的存在。

James Clerk Maxwell found the link between electricity and magnetism, and predicted the existence of electromagnetic waves.

　　生活中有这样一种有趣的现象：当一辆警车迎面驶来的时候，听到的声音比较尖锐；而警车离去时，声音比较低沉，这就是"多普勒效应"。

　　"多普勒效应"让人们可以利用声波测量距离。麦克斯韦奠定了电磁学的基础；赫兹让人们能够更好地认识电磁波；瓦特就是根据前辈发现的理论，用电磁波测量距离，从而发明了雷达。

　　There's an interesting fact: when a police car comes to us, we hear a very sharp siren; but when it goes away, the sound drops. This is the "Doppler Effect".

　　The "Doppler Effect" allows people to measure distance with sound waves. Maxwell laid the foundation of electromagnetics; Hertz helped people better understand the electromagnetic wave; and Watt used electromagnetic waves to measure distance and invented radar based on previous theories.

雷达的工作原理
WORKING PRINCIPLE OF RADAR

雷达通过发射机和天线将电磁波发射出去，在碰到目标后，电磁波被反射回来，反射回来的电磁波被天线接收之后，将收集到的信号通过接收机输入到信号处理机里分析数据，再将得出的结论输出到显示屏。

雷达到目标的距离是根据电磁波从发射到接收所需的时间来确定的，电磁波的速度与光速一致。

$$距离 = \frac{1}{2} 光速 \times 时间$$

Radar uses a transmitter and an antenna to send out electromagnetic waves. When the waves touch the target, they are reflected. The antenna receives the reflected electromagnetic waves, and the receiver puts received signals into the signal processor for analysis. The conclusion is shown on the monitor.

The distance between radar and the target is measured by the time between sending and receiving electromagnetic waves. The speed of electromagnetic waves equals the speed of light.

Distance = 1/2 speed of light × time

想一想 Think

雷达的原理并不复杂，小朋友们，你们看懂了吗？

Are you clear about the working principle of radar now?

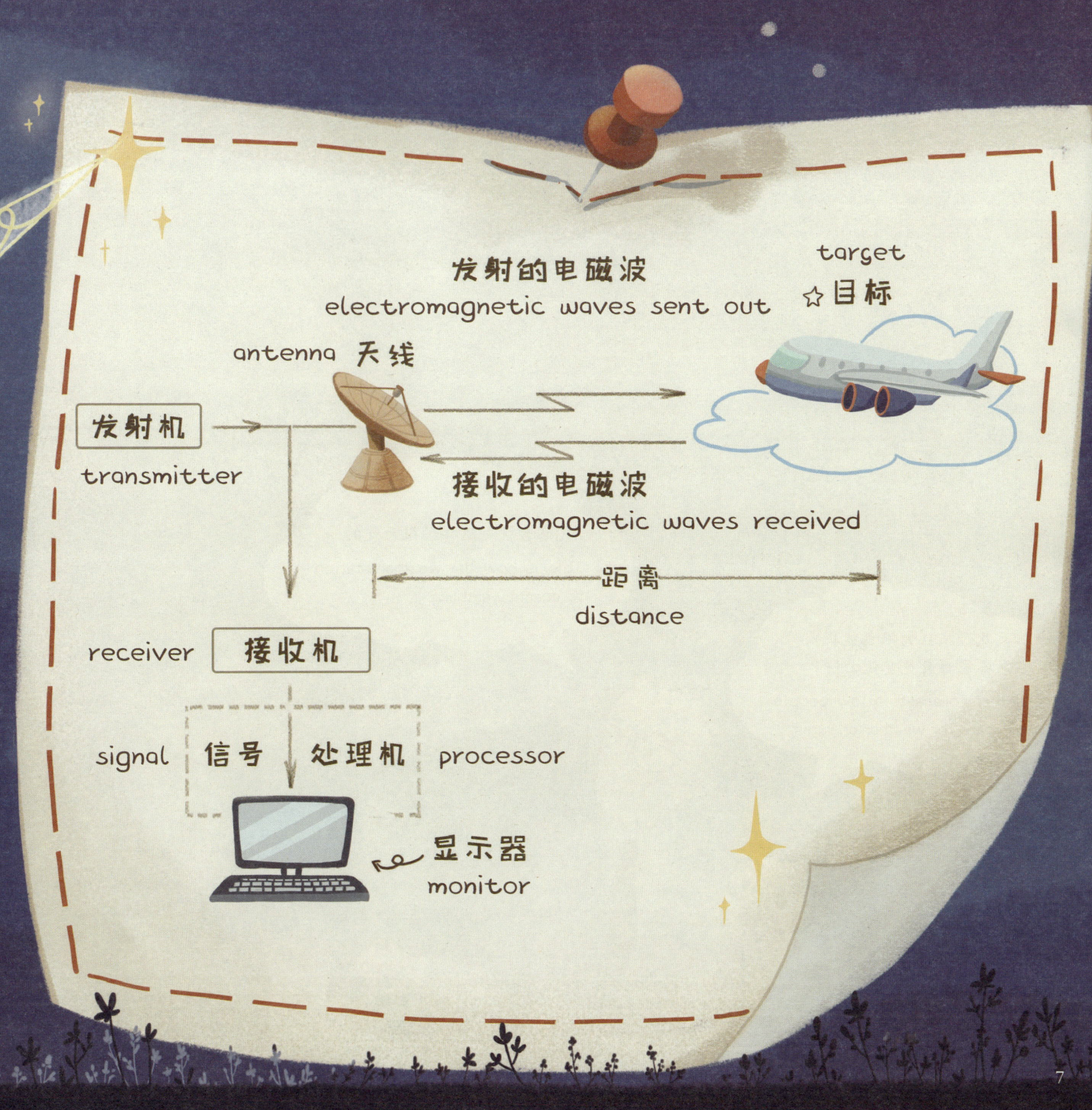

气象雷达
WEATHER RADAR

气象台就是这样预报天气的。
This is how the weather station forecasts weather.

天气预报让大家都能提前准备应对天气变化啦!
Weather forecasts allow people to prepare for weather changes.

气象雷达探测的是云、雨、暴风雪、飓风等重要的天气现象,对降水的探测是它的主要工作内容。含水的物质会将雷达发射出来的一部分信号反射回来,在一定范围内,雷达可以对这些信号进行接收。根据监测到的发射信号的强弱,可以推断出目标物体的含水量、性质、状态等,也就能预测出天气情况啦。

A weather radar detects important weather phenomena, like clouds, rain, snowstorms and hurricanes. It mainly tracks the rainfall. When radar sends out signals, objects containing water reflect part of them. In a certain range, radar can receive these signals. With the intensity of the signals, radar can find out the water content, quality and state of the target. Then, weather forecasts can be made.

不同的雷达
DIFFERENT RADARS

蜻蜓是世界上眼睛最多的昆虫之一，它的每只眼睛都由无数复眼组成，能向上、下、左、右看而不必转头。传统雷达像人类的眼睛，想看到左边，就得把头扭向左边；想看到右边，就得把头扭到右边；而相控阵雷达，相当于蜻蜓的复眼，看左边和右边都不用扭头。因此，和传统雷达相比，相控阵雷达探测和跟踪目标的速度就会快很多。

The dragonfly is one of the insects with the most eyes in the world. Each of its eyes is composed of many compound eyes, so it can look up, down, left, and right without turning its head. Traditional radar is like human eyes. It must turn left or right to see that side. A phased array radar is like the dragonfly's compound eyes. It doesn't have to turn around to look left or right. Compared with traditional radar, the phased array radar can detect and track targets much faster.

扫描方式 scanning me
天线 antenn
扫描速度 scanning s

雷达对比 Comparison of Radars

传统雷达 traditional radar	相控阵雷达 phased array radar
机械扫描 mechanical	电子扫描 electronic
靠旋转天线扫描 turning antenna	静止不动，靠电子波束 using electron beams without turning
每分钟转动5~6圈，对一个目标扫描一次大约需要10秒，确立一个目标并建立跟踪航迹需要3~6次扫描，一共30~60秒 turning 5-6 rounds per minute, around 10 seconds for scanning one target, and 30-60 seconds for 3-6 scans to locate a target and track it	从确立一个目标到建立跟踪航迹只需要几秒 seconds from locating a target to tracking it

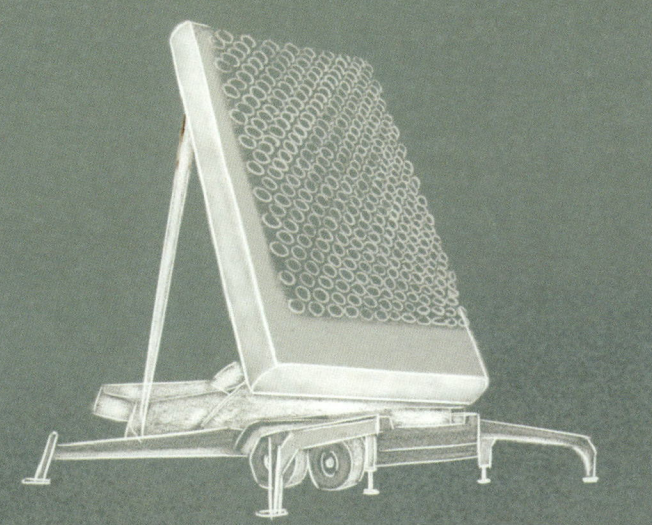

860 炮瞄雷达与空警-2000 预警机
860 FIRE-CONTROL RADAR AND AIRBORNE-2000 EARLY WARNING AIRCRAFT

860 炮瞄雷达，是我国 20 世纪 60 年代研制的火炮控制雷达，采用的是传统机械扫描方式。它在 20 世纪 90 年代中期以前是我国主要的炮瞄雷达之一。这一系列雷达车曾在战场上协助我军击落大量敌机。

860 Fire-Control Radar was the fire-control radar developed in the 1960s in China. It used the traditional mechanical scanning. Before the mid-1990s, it was one of the major fire-control radars in China. This series of radar vehicles helped the Chinese army shoot down many enemy aircraft.

空警-2000预警机是用于空中预警与指挥控制的飞机,搭载的是相控阵雷达。它由俄罗斯伊尔-76运输机改装,加装中国自主研发的相控阵雷达、碟形天线等硬件及软件。空警-2000主要担负空中巡逻警戒、监视、识别、跟踪空中和海上目标,指挥引导战机和地面防空武器系统作战等任务。

The Airborne-2000 Early Warning Aircraft was used for airborne early-warning and commanding. It was loaded with the phased array radar. It was converted from the Russian Ilyushin IL-76 transport aircraft, and was loaded with the phased array radar and the dish antenna developed by China. The Airborne-2000 was mainly responsible for air patrol, surveillance, identification, and tracking targets in air and at sea. It commanded combat aircrafts and ground air defense weapon systems for operations and other tasks.

中国雷达的发展历程
DEVELOPMENT OF RADAR IN CHINA

我国的雷达技术好厉害啊！
China's radar technology is amazing!

第二阶段
仿制阶段（1953—20世纪60年代初）
以建立雷达生产基地和仿制苏式雷达产品为主，扩展了我国部队装备雷达产品的门类，形成了雷达为陆海空部队服务的雏形。

Phase Two
Replicating (1953–early 1960s)
China mainly built radar production bases, replicated Soviet radar products, made more types of military radar products, and formed the early radar service for the army, the navy, and the air force.

第一阶段
修配阶段（1949—1953）
1949年5月，人民解放军接管了原国民党政府雷达研究所，雷达工业发展正式起步。

Phase One
Repairing & Replacing (1949–1953)
In May 1949, the People's Liberation Army took over the Radar Repair Institute from the Kuomintang government. The radar industry started its real development.

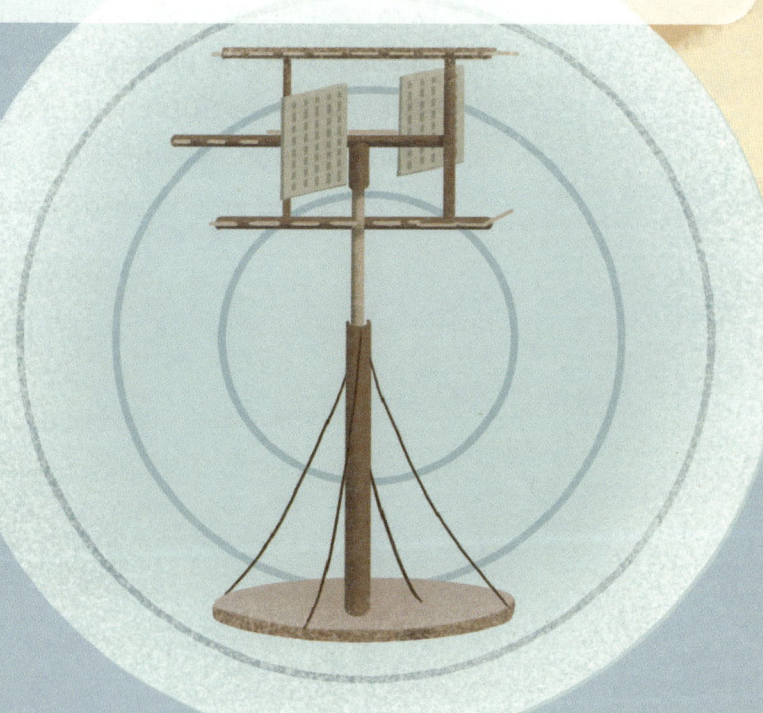

中国雷达的发展也是经历多个阶段，一步一步走过来的哦！
The development of radar in China went through several phases.

第三阶段

自行设计阶段（20世纪60年代初—70年代中期）
雷达生产脱离了国外产品的图纸、工艺资料和样机，但是整机所需的原料、元器件和部件还要依赖国外。

Phase Three

Independent Designing (early 1960s–mid 1970s)
China's radar production no longer relied on foreign designs, technologies, or prototypes. But the raw materials, components and spare parts still came from abroad.

第四阶段

发展提高阶段（20世纪70年代中期以后）
雷达技术不断突破，品种增多，实现"军民结合"，自主生产的雷达进入了国际市场。

Phase Four

Accelerating (since mid 1970s)
China's radar technology keeps making breakthroughs and producing a wider range of products. Radar has been applied to both military and civilian fields. The independently produced radars are entering the international market.

雷达的应用
APPLICATION OF RADARS

预警雷达 early warning radar

炮瞄雷达 fire-control radar

雷达一开始被发明就是作为军用装备，后来才慢慢走入了民用领域，造福更多的普通人。

Radar was first invented for military use, but later slowly entered the civilian field. It brings more convenience to people.

舰载雷达 shipborne radar

自动驾驶 automatic driving

车载雷达 vehicle radar

气象雷达 weather radar

你还知道哪些呢?
What else do you know?

哇,原来雷达有这么多用途!
Wow, radar can be so useful!

尾声
THE END

结束了雷达世界的参观之旅，小科回到家后，看到电视里的战机飞过，小科想起今天学到的知识，不禁为祖国强大的军事力量感到高兴。

Kyle comes back home after the tour in the radar world. When he sees the warplanes flying on TV, he recalls the knowledge he learns today, and feels very happy for the great military power of the motherland.